Natural Disasters

DROUGHT

Terry Jennings

Thameside Press

U.S. publication copyright © 2000 Thameside Press
International copyright reserved in all countries.
No part of this book may be reproduced in any form
without written permission from the publisher.

Distributed in the United States by
Smart Apple Media
123 South Broad Street
Mankato, Minnesota 56001

Text copyright © Terry Jennings 1999

Produced for Thameside Press by Bender Richardson White
Editors: Lionel Bender and Clare Oliver
Designer: Ben White
Electronic makeup: Mike Weintroub
Illustrator: Rudi Vizi
Picture researchers: Cathy Stastny and Daniela Marceddu
Consultant: Stephen Watts

Printed in Singapore

ISBN: 1-929298-45-5
Library of Congress Catalog Card Number 99-71376

10 9 8 7 6 5 4 3 2 1

Words in **bold** appear in the glossary on pages 30 and 31.

Contents

Rain and drought

No one likes to get caught in the pouring rain. Rain can ruin a day out and makes walking to school miserable. It can even flood streets, roads, railroads, and homes. But we all need rain if we are to stay alive. We need it to water the crops that we grow for food and to provide us with clean water for drinking, washing, and cooking.

When no rain falls

A **drought** is a long period of dry weather when no rain falls for weeks, months, or even years. Many parts of the world expect drought every year. These are places that have a dry season and a wet season. People plan for the drought by storing water and by growing crops that can withstand the dry weather.

▼ Deserts have drought all the time, but unexpected droughts happen most often in hot places such as Southeast Asia, Australia, and Central and Southern Africa.

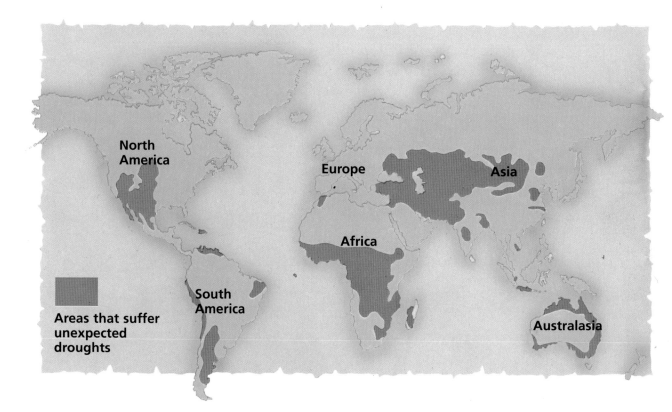

North America

Europe

Asia

Africa

South America

Australasia

Areas that suffer unexpected droughts

Surprise drought

Drought is far worse when it is not expected. In tropical areas, if the rains fail, then there is no water to store for the dry season.

Drought makes lakes, rivers, **reservoirs**, and wells dry up. Plants shrivel and die. Animals trample the ground as they search for plants to eat and water to drink. Strong winds may blow away the **topsoil**. In the hot sun, the dry plants may catch fire. Then, there is no new growth of plants.

▼ *In countries such as Burkina Faso, water is in short supply. These children collect water from a well that has been dug into a dry riverbed.*

▲ *Plants, such as this crop of sugar beet, wither and die during a drought.*

With no crops for food, people starve unless they can get food from somewhere else. In the poorer countries of the world, drought brings **famine**, disease, and death on a huge scale.

Living with drought

In this book we look at where rain comes from and how and why the rains sometimes fail. We see the effects of drought on people, plants, animals, and the landscape. We also discover why droughts are becoming more common, and what we can do to prevent them.

What is rain?

Rain and **clouds** are important parts of the **water cycle**. This is the process that allows us to use the same water over and over again. Heat from the Sun changes water from oceans, lakes, seas, trees, the soil, and other moist surfaces into an invisible gas called **water vapor**. This process of forming water vapor is known as **evaporation**.

The water vapor rises in the atmosphere. As it does so, it cools. This makes the vapor **condense** into tiny water droplets which we see as clouds. Sometimes, clouds may be made of ice crystals too.

Rain and snow

The clouds that produce rain are those in which the air is rising. If the rising air **currents** are strong, the water droplets bump into each other and form larger drops which may be big enough to fall as rain. Snowfall happens in the same way, but this time ice crystals,

▼ *Most rain falls straight back into the oceans. The rain that falls on land may drain into rivers and eventually be carried back to the sea.*

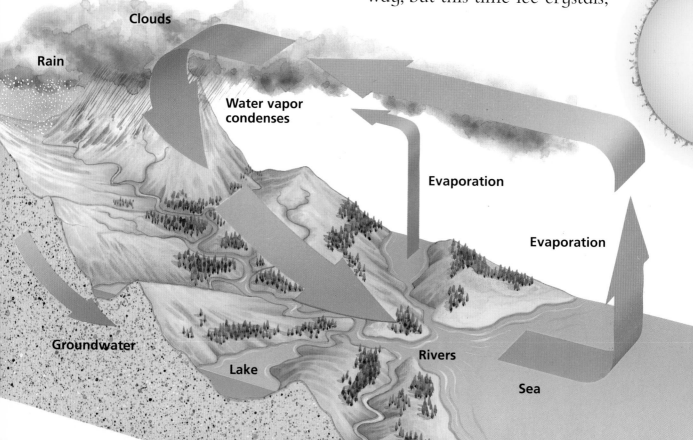

Clouds

Rain

Water vapor condenses

Evaporation

Evaporation

Groundwater

Lake

Rivers

Sea

not droplets, join together to make snowflakes. If the snow passes through warm air as it falls, it melts into rain. Otherwise, it falls as snow.

▼ *This picture of the Earth, taken by a satellite in space, shows bands of clouds. These bring rain to different parts of the Earth's surface.*

Why the rains fail

Anything that interrupts the water cycle can produce a drought. It may be that the winds change direction, causing rain-bearing clouds to travel elsewhere. This may cause unexpected flooding in one area and drought in another area.

Sometimes an area of high **air pressure** settles in one place for a long time. Then, the air becomes very still and calm. This prevents any rain clouds forming and can lead to drought.

Droughts can be caused by the tiniest change in **temperature** of the surface of the sea, or higher than average air temperatures. If the surface water becomes warmer, there is less evaporation of the sea and so fewer clouds form.

▼ *In hot, sunny places, moisture evaporates from the land. At the same time, the air is warmed and begins to rise. Upward air currents make the moist air cool and clouds start to form.*

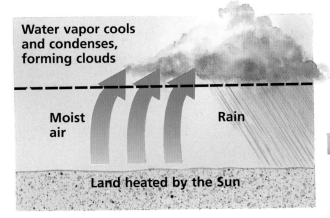

Water vapor cools and condenses, forming clouds

Moist air

Rain

Land heated by the Sun

▼ *Mountains force moist winds from the sea to rise and cool. The clouds grow until rain falls on the windward side of the mountains. Areas on the sheltered (leeward) side are often dry.*

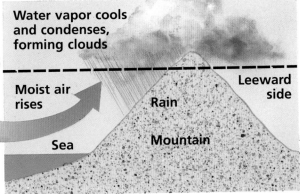

Water vapor cools and condenses, forming clouds

Moist air rises

Rain

Leeward side

Sea

Mountain

How drought begins

◄ *During a long drought, wild and domestic animals die of starvation and lack of water. This giraffe died during a drought in Kenya.*

Lack of rain leads to serious water shortages. In areas such as North Africa, Southeast Asia, and the Midwest of the United States, regular **climate** changes bring droughts that can last for years.

Types of drought

Deserts have drought all the time. This is called permanent drought. But desert peoples are used to the dry conditions and are experts at surviving in the harsh environment.

Other places have regular rainy and dry seasons. Droughts here are predictable too. The countries around the Mediterranean Sea, for example, have rains in winter and droughts in summer.

Causes of drought

No one knows for certain why droughts happen. They could be affected by ocean currents, by how moist the soil is, or by the shape of the land.

In the United States, some deserts are on the **leeward** side of mountains, where no rain-carrying winds reach them. The Kalahari and Sahara deserts in Africa are so far inland that no rains reach them.

Often when a drought does finally end, there is a severe storm and heavy rain. Water rushes over the hard, dry surface, washing away the topsoil. This makes it even more difficult to grow grass or crops again in the future.

Are people to blame?

If people take too much water from wells, rivers, and lakes, they can make a drought more serious than it would otherwise be. People also make the effects of drought worse by farming the land badly, or by letting too many animals feed on grassland.

As you can read later, we are all responsible for one of the causes of drought, wherever we live, because of the many ways we pollute our air.

▲ *Here in Thailand, a drought has dried out the soil. The plants have died and the ground is parched and cracked.*

▼ *Some deserts, like the Nevada Desert in the United States, are separated from rain-carrying winds by mountain ranges. All the rain falls on the windward side of the mountain.*

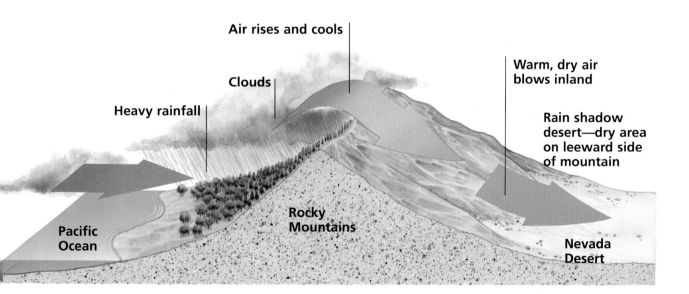

Air rises and cools

Clouds

Heavy rainfall

Warm, dry air blows inland

Rain shadow desert—dry area on leeward side of mountain

Pacific Ocean

Rocky Mountains

Nevada Desert

Climate change

▲ *Today, the Sahara Desert is one of the hottest, driest places on Earth.*

▼ *This ancient engraving of people with their cattle shows that the Sahara was once green and fertile.*

The world's climate is changing. It has always done this, but in the past it changed very slowly. Thousands of years ago, places that are now desert were lush and green, because they received rain.

Ancient art

Today the Sahara Desert is one of the hottest, driest places on Earth. But people have discovered cave paintings in the Sahara that were made about 8,000 years ago. They show flowing rivers where crocodiles and hippopotamuses lived. There are grassland animals, such as elephants, giraffes, and antelopes, as well as pictures of people driving cattle.

Drying out

About 3,000 years ago the climate began to change, and the heavy rain stopped. The land began to dry out. The grass no longer grew so well. Sheep, cattle, goats, and other animals nibbled away the remaining grass, leaving bare soil. Then the soil blew away, leaving only rocks and sand.

Desert and semidesert

The Sahara Desert does not end abruptly, but gradually changes. The region to the south of the desert is known as the **Sahel**, an Arabic word for "shoreline." It is an area of semidesert and patchy dry grass, where the average rainfall is only 4 to 8 inches a year.

Unpredictable rainfall

Some years, the Sahel region has good rainfall, then these are followed by years of drought. Between 1950 and 1967, the rainfall seemed to be increasing. Local farmers plowed land nearer to the Sahara and planted crops there. Herdsmen took their sheep, goats, and camels farther into the desert.

But the good years were followed by a drought that lasted from 1968 until the 1980s. This drought, the worst in 150 years, caused terrible famines and led to the deaths of millions of people.

▼ *The Sahel region includes parts of Senegal, Mauritania, Mali, Niger, Burkina Faso, and Chad.*

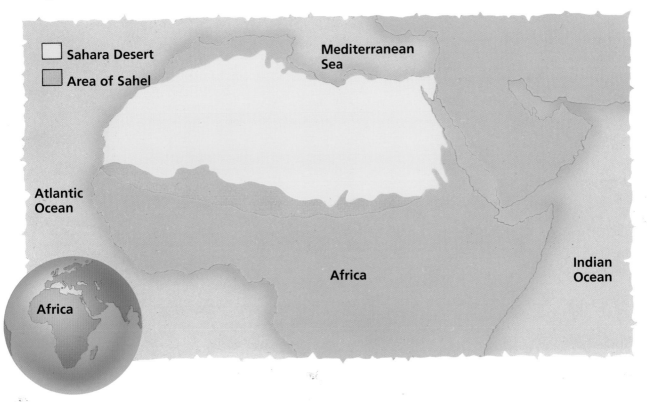

Sahara Desert

Area of Sahel

Mediterranean Sea

Atlantic Ocean

Africa

Indian Ocean

Africa

A dry world?

Energy from the Sun is absorbed by the Earth as heat. Most of this heat is radiated away from the Earth, where some of it warms the air above. **Carbon dioxide** and other gases in the air trap some of this heat. If they didn't, the whole world would be a frozen wasteland.

Now we are putting extra carbon dioxide into the atmosphere, for example when we burn fuels. As a result, more of the Sun's energy is being trapped and the world is gradually getting warmer.

The greenhouse effect

In many ways, carbon dioxide gas in the atmosphere acts like the glass roof of a greenhouse. That is why carbon dioxide is often called a greenhouse gas, and the way it is raising the temperature of the air above the Earth is called the **greenhouse effect**.

▼ *Carbon dioxide from factories, power stations, motor vehicle exhausts, and forest fires builds up in the atmosphere and traps the Sun's heat.*

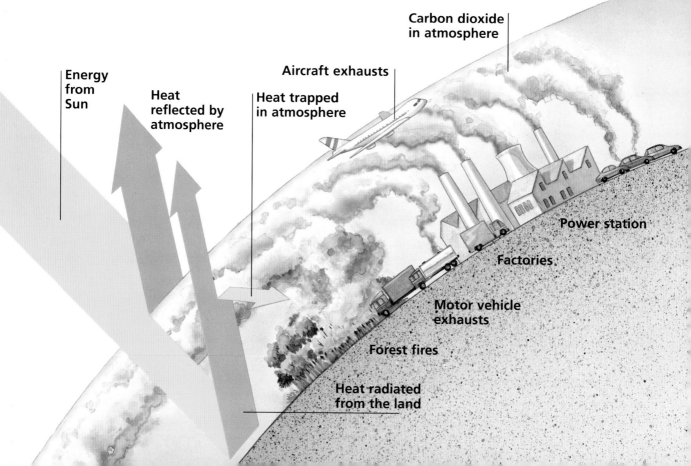

Carbon dioxide in atmosphere

Energy from Sun

Heat reflected by atmosphere

Heat trapped in atmosphere

Aircraft exhausts

Power station

Factories

Motor vehicle exhausts

Forest fires

Heat radiated from the land

Global warming

Already the average world temperature has risen by almost 2°F since 1850. Many scientists believe that the temperature could rise another 3.5°F by the year 2100.

A flooded world

This does not sound much, but if it happens, the huge layers of ice and snow at the North and South Poles will begin to melt, causing sea levels to rise by 20 inches. Low-lying land, including many of the world's largest cities, will be flooded. The patterns of the world climate will change too. There will be more droughts and many parts of the world will become so dry that crops will not be able to grow.

▲ *Power stations produce electricity by burning fuels such as oil, coal, or gas. They release huge amounts of carbon dioxide into the atmosphere.*

▼ *Global warming will cause sea levels to rise, so that low-lying islands may be flooded.*

El Niño

El Niño is a current of warm water in the Pacific Ocean. Its name is Spanish for "the child" and was given because the current usually affects the coast of Peru each Christmas. But every two to seven years, El Niño flows farther south, causing drastic changes to the climate in many parts of the world.

Normal behavior

In a normal year, El Niño warms the western side of the Pacific Ocean. The waters there may be more than 18°F warmer than those on the eastern side. Over the water the air pressure is low.

▼ *Wichita, in the United States, suffered a drought because of El Niño in February 1996. Dust particles in the air from forest fires created this beautiful sunset.*

◄ *El Niño brings severe drought to New South Wales, Australia. Heat waves, blinding dust storms, and wildfires add to the problems caused by lack of water.*

The lighter, moist air rises and brings clouds and heavy rain to Southeast Asia, New Guinea, and northern Australia.

On the eastern side of the Pacific Ocean, the seawater is cold and the air pressure is high. Few clouds form, so there is little rain along the western coasts of South America.

At the same time, the trade winds blow from east to west, pushing the sun-warmed waters westward.

Reverse weather

When an El Niño event occurs, and the current flows farther south, the cold area in the eastern Pacific and the warm western area swap over. The trade winds reverse their direction, too. On the western side of the Pacific, no rain falls, and Australia, Indonesia, and Borneo suffer drought. There are droughts, too, in India and in the Sahel, southern Africa, and Brazil.

Floods and typhoons

While there are droughts in some parts of the world, the warm water off the coast of South America produces extra rainfall that causes damaging floods and mudslides in northern Peru, Ecuador, and the state of California. The warm water produces typhoons and hurricanes in the Pacific, too.

Causing chaos

No one really knows what makes El Niño sometimes behave differently. Some scientists believe that the greenhouse effect is the cause. Recent El Niño reverses began in 1984, 1991, 1994, and 1997. The effects of the changed pattern can last up to four years.

The El Niño event of 1997 was the most violent of this century. Indonesia and other parts of Southeast Asia suffered the worst drought in 50 years, followed by massive forest fires. Australia also suffered drought and bushfires.

▲ *This forest fire in Kalimantan, Indonesia, was caused by the El Niño event of 1997–1998.*

Desertification

▲ In desert areas, such as here in Tunisia, strong winds soon bury crops if they are not sheltered by bushes and trees.

All over the world, the desert is spreading. Some scientists believe that more than 40 square miles of land become desert each day. This process, where fertile land becomes desert, is called **desertification**. It threatens about a third of the world's land surface. Deserts are spreading not only because of global warming, but also because of the way people treat the land.

Overgrazing

The areas most affected lie around the true deserts. These are known as **arid**, **semiarid** or semidesert lands. These lands turn into desert as the number of people living there increases. All these extra people need food, clothing, water, and homes. To supply the growing population, vast areas of grassland are cleared for farming, or are grazed and trampled by domestic animals.

► Goats will eat almost any plant life, so they are cheap to keep. But when goats eat too many plants, they can help create desert conditions.

Because of this land use, there is no vegetation to stop rainwater running away. If it does rain, the water runs off the surface of the land before it has had time to sink into the soil.

Caring for the soil

African farmers used to be able to cope with poor soils and irregular rains. They did not grow the same crop on the same piece of land two years running. They also rested very poor soils for up to 20 years before replanting them. But with so many more people to feed, it is no longer possible to rest the soil.

The importance of trees

In many parts of the world, people use trees for firewood, because they have no other fuels. But in times of drought, people cut down trees faster than new ones can grow. This is because people have no other food to feed their animals, so they have to give them leaves and twigs.

Without tree roots to bind the soil together, the dry soil blows away in the wind. But steps are being taken locally to stop the spread. Shrubs are being planted to hold the soil together, and lines of stones are being placed on the ground to stop rainwater draining away quickly.

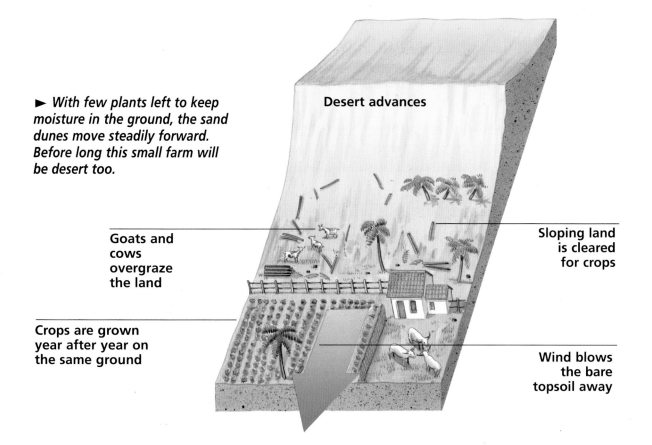

► *With few plants left to keep moisture in the ground, the sand dunes move steadily forward. Before long this small farm will be desert too.*

Desert advances

Goats and cows overgraze the land

Sloping land is cleared for crops

Crops are grown year after year on the same ground

Wind blows the bare topsoil away

Famine

A long drought often leads to famine. A famine is when a large number of people do not have enough to eat. The hot Sun kills the crops and dries up water supplies. Animals kept for meat and milk either starve to death or have to be killed. The small amount of water that is still available is often dirty and full of germs.

Soil erosion
When crops fail in a drought, the dry topsoil is left exposed to the air. It becomes as dry as dust and is blown away by strong winds. This

▲ *A relief center provides help for Sudanese children during the famine of 1994. Richer countries can help by providing famine victims with food and medicines.*

makes it even more difficult to grow crops when the rain returns, so there is even less food for the people to eat in the future.

Suffering people
When people do not have enough to eat, they are weak and cannot fight off disease. This is particularly true of children and old people. Babies die as their mothers' milk dries up. Children and adults starve.

Starvation in the Sahel

The Sahel region of Africa suffered a severe drought in the 1980s. This led to a terrible famine. Ethiopia was the most badly hit. Usually, during a drought, food can be brought in from areas where rains have watered the crops. But in 1980, no rain fell at all in Ethiopia, and over half of the country's cattle died. Ethiopia was too poor to buy food from other countries.

During the famine, a long and violent civil war prevented food reaching the people in greatest need. About two million people died of starvation.

▲ *This village in the Sahara Desert region of Chad was abandoned. It was impossible to grow crops because of the advancing sand dunes.*

▲ *During the Ethiopian famine in the 1980s, foreign aid organizations brought in truckloads of food supplies.*

Monsoon failure

Another severe drought struck the state of Orissa, in India, in 1998. There had already been several years of very little rain, but that year the **monsoon** rains failed to arrive at all. Scientists think this was because of El Niño.

Crops withered and died, and more than half a million people were forced to leave their homes and move to other areas where they could find food. Many more starved to death.

The Dust Bowl

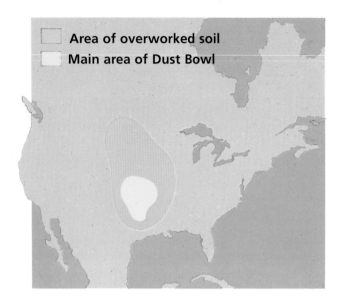

Area of overworked soil
Main area of Dust Bowl

▲ *During a drought in the 1930s, much of the Great Plains region in the United States was turned into a dry area called the Dust Bowl.*

▼ *The Great Plains area looked like this before people plowed up the grassland to grow crops.*

One of the most famous areas that has suffered drought is the Dust Bowl, an area of the Great Plains in the United States.

As in the Sahel region of Africa, people started to farm new land there during the years when there was more rain than usual. When there was a period of drought, the crops died and many people suffered severe hardship.

Intensive farming

Originally, the Great Plains were grasslands. Grasses held the fine soil in place, even though long droughts often affected the area.

Then, in the early part of the twentieth century, thousands of farmers settled in the region. They plowed up the grass and planted cereal crops, such as wheat and corn. They also raised cattle.

Soil turns to powder

To earn more money from the land, the farmers grew crops year after year, instead of letting the land rest for some years. With little or no time to recover, the overworked soil gradually became drier and even more powdery.

Dust storms

In the early 1930s, the Great Plains region suffered a period of severe drought. For five years there was no rain. In 1934 a gale swept across the United States and picked up some 400,000 tons of dust. Birds suffocated in midair. Cities such as New York were plunged into darkness when clouds of dust blotted out the Sun.

Thousands of farms were ruined, and more than 350,000 people had to abandon their homes. Thousands more died of starvation, or of lung diseases caused by breathing air that was full of dust.

Better ways to farm

In 1935 the American government began to try to improve what had become known as the Dust Bowl. Some land was planted with special grasses to bind the soil. Crops were sown in **rotation** so that they did not damage the soil, and fields were rested every third year. Hedges and rows of trees were planted to break the force of the wind. Reservoirs were built to store water. Despite this, every ten years, there have still been droughts and destructive dust storms.

▼ *During the 1930s drought, many farmers had to leave their homes in the Great Plains.*

Storms and devils

Droughts often cause dust storms, like those in the Dust Bowl. During dry spells, strong winds whip up the parched soil into swirling clouds of dust. The land becomes less and less fertile each time more soil is blown away.

Dust storms

Dust storms and sandstorms occur when high winds sweep up the loose dust and sand from the ground and swirl it about. A dust storm can be up to 400 miles wide and lift the dust to heights of 14,000 feet. It can shift millions of tons of dust or sand in just a few hours. Dust from the Sahara Desert has even been blown to the United Kingdom and parts of South America.

Dust destruction

During a dust storm, you cannot see more than 400 yards ahead. The air is so thick with dust that nothing can breathe. The dust and sand piles up in heaps, some more

▼ *A sandstorm strikes in Algeria. The sand is blinding to anyone caught in the storm. In desert areas, sandstorms can rage for several days.*

▲ *After a sandstorm, people who live in desert areas often have to dig out their houses.*

Whirling devils

Dust devils, or whirlwinds, are spinning funnels of flying dust. Their energy comes from the heat of the ground. They may form anywhere, but most occur in hot, desert and semidesert regions.

In the Sahara Desert, there are dust devils lasting from five minutes to a few hours, every day. In Tucson, a desert city in the state of Arizona, there are about 80 dust devils every day. The largest dust devil ever occurred in the state of Utah. It was almost 2,500 feet high and traveled 40 miles in seven hours.

than 13 feet high. These block roads and railroads. Windows are sandblasted into sheets of frosted glass, and paintwork is worn away. Even after the winds drop, the dust may stay suspended in the air for days. It filters the Sun's rays and creates beautiful sunsets.

Dust storms also remove valuable soil from farmland. Each year, farmers in the United States lose 20 million tons of soil to dust storms and in Russia, a million acres of farmland are ruined.

► *A dust devil whips up a towering spiral of dust, soil, and garbage.*

Wildfires

▲ *Australia suffers some of the world's worst wildfires. Oils in the country's most common tree, the eucalyptus, help to fuel the flames.*

Wildfires are frequent during a drought, because plants become very dry. Hot, dry winds fan the flames.

Some wildfires are started by lightning, but most are caused by people. Usually a wildfire begins because of a careless accident, but a few fires are lit deliberately.

Useful fires

Although fires damage crops, they can be useful. Fires burn up dried plants and deadwood and clear gaps in forests where new seedlings can grow. After a fire in the African savanna, green shoots appear, providing food for grazing animals. Some plants, such as the eucalyptus and the banksia shrub in Australia, rely on fire to release the seeds from their pods.

Burning out

Most fires that are started by a flash of lightning are eventually put out by rain. They may die out when they reach water or an area where there is little material to burn. But if a wildfire is not controlled very quickly, it can rage across the countryside, causing widespread and serious damage and loss of life.

Deadly fumes

Fires also pollute the air with their smoke. In 1997 and 1998, Indonesia and Malaysia suffered the worst drought in 50 years. People had been using fires to clear areas of forest. Unfortunately, the monsoons did not come to put out the fires. The fires burned out of control for months, covering Southeast Asia with smoke and fumes.

▲ *Forest fires raged through southern France and Spain during the summer of 1997. Special aircraft were used to drop water and fire-damping chemicals onto the wildfires.*

▲ *Forest fires swept through parts of California in 1997 and 1998, destroying homes and setting on fire household gas and oil supplies.*

Fighting the flames

Firefighters use a wide range of equipment to put out wildfires, including mobile pumps, water tankers, and bulldozers. They may attack a fire directly by spraying water or chemicals onto it or by beating out the flames.

Special fixed-wing aircraft and helicopters dump huge quantities of water onto the fire. Often, firefighters clear all the vegetation around the fire, to stop the flames spreading any farther.

Shrinking seas

People can create drought conditions by disrupting the water cycle. The Aral Sea is an inland sea on the borders of Kazakhstan and Uzbekistan in Central Asia. It was once the fourth-largest inland sea in the world, covering 26,000 square miles. In the last ten years, it has shrunk to half its size.

A natural reservoir

The Aral Sea used to be a natural reservoir in a vast, desert area. Its waters helped to improve the local climate. Today, over 75 percent of its water has evaporated. In some places there are fishing villages that lie 50 miles away from the water. Fishing boats have been left high and dry. The fish died because the salt **concentrated** in the seawater as the water evaporated.

Disastrous ditches

The Aral Sea began drying up in the 1960s. This was because people changed the direction of the two rivers that flowed into the Aral Sea.

▼ *When the Aral Sea began to dry up, ships were left on dry ground. The fishing industry has been destroyed, with a loss of 60,000 jobs.*

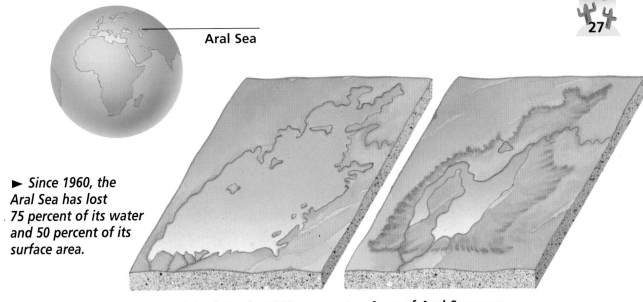

Aral Sea

► *Since 1960, the Aral Sea has lost 75 percent of its water and 50 percent of its surface area.*

Area of Aral Sea in 1960

Area of Aral Sea now

The people channeled the water onto their fields. But the **irrigation** ditches were badly made. The soil became waterlogged and the crops of cotton and rice could not grow.

Changing climate

Since the 1960s, the climate around the Aral Sea has also changed. Summers are hotter and winters are colder and longer. Each year, there are 150 days without rain, five times more than before.

Now canals have been dug to drain the land. Countries around the sea have agreed to take less water from the rivers that flow into it. But the sea will never grow to its original size again.

► *This sea of sand was once part of Lake Chad.*

Lake Chad

Lake Chad, which is in the Sahel region of Africa, was once the size of Massachusetts. Today it has shrunk to one-tenth of that.

One reason is that there has been very little rain for the last 20 years. Also, Nigeria and Cameroon have pumped so much water from the lake to try to solve their own water shortages. If nothing changes, Lake Chad will disappear in five years.

Drought prevention

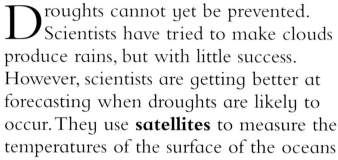

▼ *In Burkina Faso, trees are planted in a line to help hold dry soils in place. They will also take in carbon dioxide gas from the air and help reduce the greenhouse effect.*

D roughts cannot yet be prevented. Scientists have tried to make clouds produce rains, but with little success. However, scientists are getting better at forecasting when droughts are likely to occur. They use **satellites** to measure the temperatures of the surface of the oceans and to plot the progress of rain clouds. Much can also be done to try to reduce the effects of drought.

Simple devices are now being used instead of expensive machines to get the best use out of available water. This is known as appropriate or **intermediate technology**.

Tree planting

Trees can act as windbreaks, and their roots stop the soil blowing away. In some countries dry, sandy soil is sprayed with a mixture of oil and rubber to stop it blowing about. Then seedlings of acacia and eucalyptus trees, which grow fast in dry soils, are planted. The roots bind the clumps of soil firmly.

Crops grow strong in the shade and shelter of the trees, and the trees themselves eventually provide valuable wood. Also, trees absorb carbon dioxide from the air and reduce the greenhouse effect.

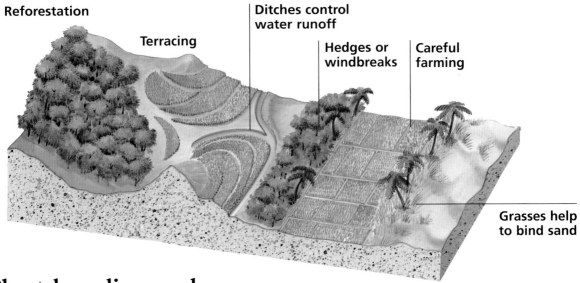

Reforestation

Terracing

Ditches control
water runoff

Hedges or
windbreaks

Careful
farming

Grasses help
to bind sand

▲ *There are many different ways to reduce the effects of drought.*

Plant breeding and manure

Scientists are trying to help reduce the effects of drought by breeding varieties of plants that can survive with little water. Already, **drought-resistant** varieties of crops such as millet and sorghum are being grown in several arid countries.

Putting animal manure and compost on dry soils helps them to hold water longer. These also bind the soil together and prevent it drying up and blowing away.

Saving water

In places where drought is likely, it is important not to waste water. Reservoirs can be built to store water when it does rain. Irrigation channels can be dug to carry this water to the crops.

Terraces can be cut into sloping fields, or ridges of stones can be laid across them, to prevent rainwater from running away down slopes.

Local people need to know how to take care of their soil and not allow too many animals to graze the plants. With care, and a small amount of water, even hot, dry desert soils can grow good crops.

◄ *It is possible to grow successful crops in desert areas with proper irrigation systems, such as this one in Tunisia.*

Glossary

air pressure The weight or force of the air pressing down on the surface of the Earth.

arid A term used to describe dry land. Arid regions of the world are the deserts, where there is little rain and few plants can survive.

carbon dioxide One of the three main gases in the atmosphere, or air. The others are oxygen and nitrogen.

climate The average weather of a region of the Earth throughout the year.

cloud A group of many millions of tiny water droplets or ice crystals in the sky.

concentrated When something is strong because it is mixed with only a little water, such as some medicines that need to be diluted. Seawater becomes concentrated with salt as some of the water evaporates.

condense To cool water vapor so that it turns back to liquid water.

current The movement of air or water in a particular direction.

desert A dry region with very few plants.

desertification The process in which once fertile land is turned into desert. The land cannot easily be made fertile again.

drought An unusually long period of dry weather.

drought-resistant Describes something, such as a plant, that is able to survive well in drought conditions.

dust devil A small whirlwind, carrying dust and sand, that forms over the land on hot, sunny days.

dust storm A strong wind that sweeps along large quantities of dust and sand.

El Niño The shifting of warm water and a wet climate from the western to the eastern side of the Pacific Ocean. This leads to major changes in the weather around the world.

evaporation When water is heated it disappears into the air as water vapor. This is called evaporation.

famine A time when there is not enough food for the people of an area.

fertile Land that is fertile has a rich soil and produces good crops.

greenhouse effect The warming of the Earth caused by carbon dioxide and other gases in the air that reduce the amount of the Sun's heat that escapes back into space.

intermediate technology Methods of technology that are neither very simple nor very complex, but make the most use of local resources and skills and do not damage the environment.

irrigation Taking water from rivers, lakes, wells, or reservoirs and channeling it along ditches or putting it onto the land so that crops grow well.

leeward The side of a hill or mountain that is sheltered from the wind.

monsoon A wind that blows from the land in winter. In summer it changes direction and blows from the Indian Ocean, bringing heavy rains to southern Asia.

reservoir A large artificial lake used to store water for drinking, producing electricity, and watering crops or to prevent a river flooding.

rotation To grow a different crop each year on a plot of land so that the soil does not become worn out.

Sahel The belt of dry, semiarid land at the southern edge of the Sahara Desert.

satellite A satellite is something that moves around something larger, as the Earth moves around the Sun. We send man-made satellites into orbit around the Earth to collect information about the weather.

semiarid The lands around the deserts are said to be semiarid because, although they are dry, they receive a little more rainfall than the deserts do.

temperature The measure of how hot or cold something is.

terrace One of a series of level areas on a slope or hillside that look like huge steps.

topsoil The top, fertile layer of the soil. It contains the goodness that plants need if they are to grow healthily.

water cycle The circulation of the Earth's water, in which it evaporates from the sea, lakes, rivers, and other moist surfaces to the air. It then cools and turns back into rain, sleet, or snow which falls to the Earth below.

water vapor The gas that forms when water is heated.

wildfire A fire that burns grassland, forest, scrub, bush, or other wild plant life.

windward The side of a hill or mountain facing the wind; the opposite to leeward.

Index